Audacity to Stand:
How to Protect Victims of Abuse from Themselves

Oludare O Eniwaye Ph.D. HS-BCP © 2018

www.amazon.com

Dedication

This book is dedicated everyone in this blue jewel in space that are trodden down, used and abused by perpetrators; When the Ron's of the world try to run you down thinking you have no way out. Do not lose hope and never give up because your deliverance is at hand.

Contents

PREFACE

BASIC PRICIPLES FOR WORKING WITH PEOPLE IN A COUNSELING RELATIONSHIP

1. We assume that people are capable or potentially capable. If people currently lack insight, knowledge, and skills, we as professionals are responsible to help them become insightful, knowledgeable and skillful.

2. We reject the traditional methods of practice that assume that the problem with incongruent ideas lie with the person and that individuals with incongruences must change or get fixed before he or she can adequately function in the society.

3. We belief that solutions to problems faced by people are sometimes unique and probably in no uncertain terms have something in common with others; therefore, positive result rest primarily on access to society's benefit and rewards and thus, our emphasis on intervention must be political in nature.

4. We belief that even though different people may have different counseling needs, they have more in common than they have differences; therefore, practitioners need to be more knowledgeable about advocacy and referral process.

5. We belief that most people are happy with themselves and that better models of practice can enhance and improve the state of being with people with disability.

6. We believe that persons in counseling have without question, the right to control their own lives and our job is to help them find the best way to make that independence and growth more accessible.

Audacity to Stand:

Handbook on How to Protect Victims of Abuse from Themselves

Chapter 1

Types of Relationships and Counseling

You have no doubt experienced some form of relationships in your life time. The beginning and or end of relationships are determined by the foundation on which they are formed. Relationships sometimes are involuntarily conceived with certain unwritten contract-i.e. parent/child relationships, friendships formed under common interest and teacher/student relationship. While some relationships share equal responsibility for what happens either the sink or float-husband/wife relationship, how relationships will end are not always planned from the beginning.

Now, no matter how you look at it, anything with a beginning must have an end. Having said that, most relationships will eventually collapse either planned or not for many reasons, participants may not see eye-to-eye on issues regardless of advanced planning-This is the eventuality of everything. Natural order of things, cosmos transformation-- death of a participating member or neglect of duties are some of the causes of the demise of a relationship. Therefore, I reiterate relationships with a beginning must also have a finale.

In most relationships, there are one, two or three things that are bound to happen. (1) One or both people in the relationship may have nothing to prove or bring anything substantial into the relationship- therefore this type of relationship could be defined as: -- as it comes, so it goes type of relationship. (2) The other thing that might happen in a relationship is that one or both parties may be compatible to some extent, to say the least; and thus, one could make the other's life better, if this happens at the get go point, right from the beginning of the relationship-this mutual understanding creates a preferred relationship. Therefore, the relationship endures more and last longer. (3) The last happenstance in a relationship is that in which one or both in the relationship are in it to cause ruination or damage to one another; this leads to a regret and sigh confirming the obvious -the relationship should not have happened in the first place.

To be clear, like every relationship, counselor/client relationship has a beginning and a definite end. This end though is a planned one and this is most likely welcomed. Also, I would remise if I do not mention that counselor/client relationship is not an equal one. After all, one person should be congruent while the other is not. Counselor/client relationship could only be one or two mentioned above but hopefully never in the third category.

What is counseling?

Counseling is a cooperative self-improvement and preventive process that is intended to help people take more effective control of their daily lives. In counseling, thoughts and feelings are shared in confidence with someone who is objective and who is a good listener. Counselors are supposed to be the congruent part of the relationship to coordinate a discussion to help client find ways to resolve their issues.

Sometimes counseling an individual may require special assessment of the clients' emotional status in an instant in which, the person may be in a state of crisis-a state of disorganization with significant impact on important life goals. To engage clients in crisis counseling intervention, there must exist four stages of critical situations, increased tension, a demand for additional resources, and major personality disorganization that renders regular counseling impracticable (James, 2008).

Counseling process can be compared to weaving a basket. In basket weaving, you link one riff to another to achieve stronger joints and a beautiful artwork. Likewise, in counseling, the counselor asks questions based on foundational previous facts; from the answer given by the client, the counselor use part of the answer to generate a new question either to clarify or establish a new line of thought. As you continue the process, a blur vision gradually improves to a 20/20 focus.

Components of an Effective Counselor

1. Self-understanding: By this, I mean that a counselor must know where he or she is coming from before he or she can begin to tell clients where to stand, and more so understand personal idiosyncrasies' bias, feelings, and background.
2. Personal issues resolved; particularly issues related to the reason for clients in counseling.
3. Helping Profession requires Self-Sacrifice, this is the key to counselor's love for the profession

According to Decker, Scott, and Chang (2013), counselors are obligated legally and ethically to uphold the following standards: 1. Carry out professional responsibilities with an unrelenting alacrity. 2. Counselors should respect privacy of clients including physical space. Clients should not be forced to reveal more than necessary- length of time in the relationship should be considered to balance things out. 3. Have a self-sacrificing attitude toward the client by considering client individuality in the counseling process.

At this juncture, I am going to make an oxy-moron statement; decipher it as you like. Counselors, remember that It is not about you and it is about you as a counselor and better outcome of relationships may depend on full consideration of the client's worldview and the change needed in that constructivism.

Counseling Victims of Abuse

Let us get to clarity and on the same page; when the shoe is too tight, corns and calluses emerge. This is a crenelated and relevant analogy as we discuss the monstrosity of abuse. Abuse is a leviathan with many tentacles. It spreads without care and tend to grab and subject innocent victims to Ill-treatment, Mistreatment, Maltreatment, Molestation and/or Battery. Projection of this behavior is to intentionally hurt, harm and or Injure someone or a group of people who seems to have no way out of the situation or for that matter an apparent defense mechanism to avert excruciating torments and stultifying experience. There is a propensity to subject victims to some or all-out insults, name-calling, unbecoming verbal, foul language, violence, and invective blocking of escape modalities in a vitiating atmosphere.

Scales and sub scales of abuse that manifest itself in domestic violence are not homologous but have similarities that are common in romantic relationships, employee employer relationships, siblings and or strangers alike. The pervasive underground sex trade, illegal trafficking and transportation of people, modern forced labor and slavery, transportation and kidnaping and drug transactions are just a few ways of propagating models of abusive environment. From time in memoriam, people have dominated others especially if they seem not to know how to escape their oppressors. World history have shown how wicked deeds of human beings have resulted the callous treatment of fellow human beings with atrocious cruelty, enveloped in vehemently fomented brutality to inhumanly subjection with albatross repugnance.

Abuse victims who have gone through traumatic and life changing events and have been down- trodden and beaten down so much that when a repose of relief is at hand, they tend to either knowingly or unknowingly balk at the idea. Incidental or forced, victims manifest the same five stages of grief namely-denial, anger, bargaining, depression, and acceptance. To grief is one thing, but in the case of abused victims, these reactions are taken to another level, it goes further than the five stages of grief. What the abuser has done to the abused is unconscienced but that should be water under the bridge; As they say. My fear for the client is, will the enemy within be more powerful or greater than the enemy without? To be sure, there are eight road blocks of internal forces and self-deprecating doubts that deprive survivals of abuse from moving forward to that level of being free at last.

You cannot protect victims of abuse unless you understand their struggles. More importantly you can't save abused victims from their aggressors unless you get into the psyche of the abused. Don't get me wrong, counselors are not psychics but, they are blessed with the gift through the far-reaching training that enables them to develop empathy, one of the keys to unlock doors of positive change.

The problem then is that helping professionals must find ways to unlock the shame within, and invariably help victims become free from the clutch of perpetrators; and thus, may be, just maybe, the abused will shudder no more. This critical step cannot be accomplished unless there is an abundance of knowledge on what make victims resist or shy away from the help they desperately need for recovery. Invariably, this saving act, a step-hill as I call it, could turn to an up-hill battle unless professionals dig up to the foundation to locate reasons why victims seem not to respond to help with alacrity and promptly escape from their aggressors. It is equally important for counselors and other professionals to understand how to tackle victims own Achilles heel-namely resistance to therapy.

In fact, these eight items in our discussion are why people who have emerged or in transition from abusive situations seem to regress or not respond well to counseling. They (victims) may be in fact still not out of the lurch and are still petrified that abusers are in control no matter what. It takes years of training and dedication for professionals to anthropomorphize the understanding of what is needed to get abused victims out of this dreaded clutch which in turn may become a vicious circle of emotional dependence on the abused state of mind.

The helping profession have many facets, and applications are varied depending on issues, people impacted, and the need to reconcile; so, an agilely focused approach is a waste of time. Consequently, a unique problem requires unique solution and each client must be treated on the merit of individual needs. To reduce the level of recidivism, a specially carved holistic approach must be applied especially when in counseling with victims of abuse. It is therefore, the objective of this book is to familiarize professionals, counselors, therapists, law enforcement agents, and those assigned to rescue missions on dexterous ways to handle or restraint these eight shackles that could influence client's response to counseling. Lack of understanding of these diminish counselor's success and their effectiveness to helping abused victims attain desperately needed freedom.

I am a Professor but, I do not profess to know everything. But, I sincerely belief that to be fore warned is to be fore armed. These detractors as highlighted below may not manifest in the order as listed. However, a better understanding of individuals in our care should guide professionals to the best methodology of approach. You see, if you have these eight items in focus when in counseling with victims of abuse, you will certainly know what questions to ask, when to ask questions and how to reach and lead your clients to a quicker and responsive resolve of the issues and thus get to the termination and aftercare stage with ease.

Individualized case by case scrutiny suggests that people are unique in the way they handle their torture stakes; Also, be vigilant about the length of time individual client has been in the trench of turmoil you are trying to get them out of, each person's level of endurance is percolated and differs from one person to another just as night and day are differentiated.

Counselors are neither shrinking violets nor are they bulldogs. So, if you asked me how to derive joy from your well-earned career training and education, I will tell you to avail yourself to customs, values, and experiences from other cultures other than yours. Thereby, you can avoid prejudices, misconceptions, and fear that may alienate you from attaining remarkable success as a counselor. Please, avoid making a comparison of your clients with other clients who may be going through similar vices as others within the population. The solution lies in a well-designed therapeutic modality with a coordinated holistic approach. Measured care, personal and unique situations require measured response to progress in therapy. Given, every individual who comes to us for care may not ascribe to every stumbling blocks described; this can be sorted out during an

Intake. Having said that, let your training guide you to the idea that lays a bridge with the

commonality threaded in the victim's experience; to this end, be unequivocally resolved to learn

about these eight obstacles discovered, and prepare to ask questions relevant to which of these are

topical with your client, then focus on them for the sake of saving you and your clients time and

headache. Word of caution, although it is very rear for every client to be in a quick sand with all

the eight scenarios in our discussion, you the professional needs to know how to win your clients

over should he or she have a struggle with any of them.

Chapter 2

Eight Blocking Huddles in the Way of Abused Victims Success

1. Identifies with their abusers

What do you say to victims who seem not to want your help or involuntarily is reluctant to shed information that could help you help them?   Sometimes an abusive relationship starts in a methodical, deliberate, and a gradual progressive entanglement. On the other hand, abusers may start chivalrously through implicit threat, manipulation, coercion or forced direct intimidation. Once these acts take effect, just like the red head lizard, the abuser may change tactics by seemingly becoming nice to the abused and probably convince him or her that there is a good reason for cooperation. It is at this stage the victim tends to identify with the abuser and invariably see the perpetrator in a different light. Victims are confused at this stage and just maybe because they have been brain-washed through a series of manipulation. And more importantly, it may be that they fear leaving a seemingly relaxed hostile environment.

Helping professionals who are working with clients at this stage should use viewpoint questions that cut through the chase. Questions should deal with client's mindset in accordance to the best direction of resolve. It is plausible to find out reasons why victims tend to see their foes as friends. Without browbeating clients, viewpoint questions may lighten the mood and possibly, they can see the predicament of their own views. It is then, and only then, a consummate professional will have a chance of helping his/her client move to the next stage needed for delivery from the jaws of the evil- namely the abuser.

2. Advocate on behalf of Perpetrators

It may sound oxy-moronic that a victim advocates for the Abuser but to be precise, there is a need for scrutiny about the victim's mind set at that juncture; understanding the peculiarity of struggles diminishes when an individual is acrimoniously written off to be too far for the center. Simply put, one needs to see within the parameters of their own rear-view mirror and clearly see what is being left behind. The longer one is victimized, the more the victim adjust to closely reflect his/her conditioned status. You see, it's not uncommon for an abused person to blame self for getting into such a predicament.

As a result, when victims are confronted with a solution-based approach and ways to get out of detrimental conditions, it is customary for abused individuals to say things, like "He or she is not that bad of a person." Make statements like, "He cannot help himself, and or "It's not her fault." When rational people who are far and removed from the middle of the situation hears analogous statements like these; they boil-over and conclude that victims must enjoy suffering or that they are mentally challenged. To be true, people who have gone through traumatic events can have their thinking process temporarily rearranged, thus, rational thinking process of individuals vaporize fleetingly and now have become irrationally motivated for however short a period. In this case, and in this instance of a moment, good is bad and bad is good.

3. Blames Themselves for their Predicament

Just imagine someone who was held against his own will for several weeks with little or no hope of getting out alive. He has endured such an ordeal and has virtually given up hope; but by a miracle, deliverance came in the nick of time. Now, everyone would like to hear his story of survival and how he has managed to stay alive. Will it not be ridiculous if this person starts his story with a-self-blame acrimony? Yet, that is exactly what happens in many of survival stories I have heard. They tend to blame themselves for being in the wrong place at the wrong time. People often whisper and label victims of abuse as carefree individuals who walks around with their eyes wide-shut. What makes it more disheartening is that victims do agree with nay-sayers.

Would it not be nice for a victim to acquiesce to a deliverance so sourly needed instead of giving abusers benefit of the doubt. On the contrary It seems that a frightened dog will only bite the rescuer no matter what. It is therefore imperative that a seasoned counselor cautiously ameliorate and expeditiously plan approach format that is determined to be successful; otherwise the keg will not only lick but also burst.

4. Appease Abusers because they are Afraid of Change

To appease the abuser could be translated in many ways namely-mollify, settle, soothe, placate, pacify, and conciliate. Abused victims sometimes cower like caged rats without realizing their actions. They may engage in this behavior to avoid provoking or accede the abuser due to fear. You see, fear is an impellent behavior which results from past memory of unpleasant experience (Eniwaye, 2014). It is this fear that stops victims in their track when they have the chance to flee from an abductor. It is like a moth running into the fire, and there is nothing good to come out it but a detrimental and unavoidable burn out.

At this moment in time, counselors and other professionals need to dig deep into the psyche of the victim to fully empathize and figure the way out of the maze. There is a need for an urgent emotional reaction by the counselor on reasons why the victim feels the perpetrator should be appeased. When counselors are emphatic with a sense of understanding and caring, a break-through in the counseling relationship should yield a desirable result.

5. Confused and Blame Helpers instead of the Abuser.

The helping profession gets blamed for many things like not being vigilant enough, acting in haste, negligence, or too heavy handed with a client or too lenient; whatever it is that need to be done, professionals must be above the fray while maintaining the fit of consummate professionals twenty-four-seven. But, what do you say to an abused victim who tells you to leave him or her alone or feels that no one understands his or her situation because no one is in their head or shoes.

More importantly, is it ok to label a victim as irrational in their thought process? I will say, it is best to keep that thought in a space not too far from your heart to get close to the point of upward trajectory and a place to work from. The middle of a ravine or quick sand is not pleasant, and it is not the time or place to dish out a blame game. But after you have rescued out someone from an environment that almost sealed off their earthly presence, then, you can point out the folly of his/her ways. Remember that confusion and irrationality is acceptable for a victim in the recovery state, but to walk lightly on the blaming side-walk belongs to the helper. If find yourself in the front end of this bit, ask the victim what can you do to help him or her see a different side of the issue. Well, this part of questioning aspect will be dealt with during the discussion of stages of the counseling process.

6. Becomes Co-dependent and Afraid to Venture out on their own.

Co-dependency is a relationship dysfunction in which a person supports or enable another person's addiction. In abusive relationships, co-dependency manifest itself through shame, guilt, low self-esteem and painful emotions accumulated from past experiences. It is not so difficult to imagine how a victim of abuse who has been stepped-on or beaten black and blue on several occasions could become so diminished to an infinitesimal state of mind; and so, they consequently are afraid to venture on their own and though unspoken, they anticipate their abusers wish becomes their command.

Professionals could be in their wits-end when dealing with an abused person who has turned co-dependent. To counter regression, Solution-based approach must graphite layers of painful emotions, self-esteem issues, guilt and shame orientations before the victim is totally consumed to the point of no-return.

7. Blocking and Transference

Blocking and Transference in this instance has to do with the abused stack of metaphysical stance in reacting to the help offered. In short, this is a problem specific to client reluctance and resistance. Blocking is a phenomenon in which previously learned behavior or thought process prevents one from moving forward to progress. You may have read other texts that explains blocking and transference differently, but be sure that my explanation in this context is absolutely accurate. Victims of abuse have been somehow conditioned to shudder when the abuser beckons. It is not unheard of that victims of abuse push repressed memory to the front thus allowing this thought process to deprive them from achieving relief as needed.

Transference on the other hand is the redirection of feelings and desires especially unconsciously retained. This redirection of thought may hinder counseling process when abused victims project or see the counselor in the same vain as the abductor or the abuser. For example, if the abuser is a male and the helper is of the same gender as the abuser, victims may create a comparison or say something like all men are the same. The comparison may not even be verbal, it may be shrugging, non-response or an overtly conjectural move back; but it will surely cause a line of demarcation between success and failure.

8. Pretends to be Rational but Object to Rational Escape Solution

"When it rains, it pours." as they say. The constant bombardment of put downs, beat downs, shut downs and shut outs has taken its toll that at this point victims are certified pretenders who are artificially insane and are ripped of irrational tendencies. At the juncture, suggestions about survival strategies and escape solutions could be a waste of time.

Remember that it is difficult to reason with someone unreasonable; therefore, therapists and counselors assigned to treat an abuse survival should always be cognizant of the fact that their clients may be in the constrict state of mind. Having said that, it is right to note that for counseling to be effective, congruency on the part of the counselor is of utmost importance; thus, counteracting the incongruency that may be anticipated as well as expected from clients.

Counselors working with abused victims must think comorbidity; Abuse takes people to the sewer of other issues like addictions, anger, co-dependency, sadness, and depression to name a few. Nevertheless, it is still in fashion to pursue counseling models that have been researched with evidence-based success rate, and more importantly in-lined with well-documented counseling stages.

Cormier and Hackney (1987) described five stages of counseling in the order of 1. Relationship Building, 2. Assessment and Diagnosis, 3. Formulation and Setting Goals, 4. Intervention and Problem Solving, 5. Termination and Follow-up. Since then, Research and Evaluation stage has been added as an impactful aspect of a successful encounter between counselors and clients in counseling relationship including abuse victims.

Lack of adequate and a well-planned intervention may lead victims of abuse to develop the following habits and or addictions: Lack of self-control, obsessive and compulsive behavior, eating disorder, workaholism, alcohol misuse, helplessness, illegal drug use, sex addiction, depression, thrill seeking behavior, nicotine dependence, relationship issues, weight control obsession, boredom, anger, Guilt, self-hate, and fear of strangers. To determine the level of need, counselors could give clients a Self-Inventory Worksheet. Counselors should also explain the meaning of each Item before clients can respond to the Inventory with an accurate objectivity.

Steps to Self-Control

Personal Self-Exam Scale (1-10)

Please write a number that denote your level of involvement on these habits or addictions

✖ Personal Self-Exam (1 – 10) Balance Point is 5; 8 and above needs Self-Control

Intervention

+ __Lack of Self-Control   __Obsessive and Compulsive Behavior

+ __ Eating Disorder   __Workaholism

+ __Alcohol Misuse   __Helplessness

+ __Illegal Drug Use   __Sex Addiction

+ __Self-Hate   __Depression

+ __Thrill Seeking Behavior   __Nicotine Dependence

+ __Relationship issues   __Anger Issues

+ __Weight Control Obsession   __Guilt Harboring

+ __Boredom   __Fear of Strangers

Strategy to Self-Control and Taking your Life back from the Abuser

Develop a Self-Talk Mantra

Then say these words aloud and repeat twice and as needed

I am the master of my life (twice)

I am in control of my own behavior (twice)

Self-Control is fun and pleasurable (twice)

I have the power and I will use it wisely (twice)

I have achieved self-control (twice)

I am a successful human being. (twice)

Chapter 3: Stages of Counseling Relationship

An abused individual who seem to have been emancipated from the abuser are still lurch prone with some huddles to jump over. He/she is still may be in a fragile position during the unquantified transition stage. Counseling and therapy are the essentials needed to improve self-control abilities, also to enhance relationship building capabilities. To be on the road to these abilities, we need to closely examine the counseling process and to determine which stage to place the client, carefully marching the individual with the stage that fits him/her; and from that stage, we can proceed forward until we get to the termination and after care stage.

Stage 1. Relationship Building

The is the stage, I call getting to know you stage; clients need a warm and genuine professional to facilitate an abundance trust and confidence in the system. A Professional must avoid façade, arrogance and omniscient attitude; otherwise, the journey of client/counselor relationship may become arduous from the beginning. Inner attributes and personality uptakes of client must be explored.

The Counselor must disinter a marvelous warm smile with an open gesture; thus, this allows a client to relax and respond well to questions from the intake session. Also, when counselor explains the relevancy of questions that seem to veer into family background, and mental status, it is easier to legitimize such questions on the form.

The easiest place to display attributes highlighted is to conduct a-well-designed intake- the intake form is on the average about 2 to 3 pages long with basic questions about the client, family history, psychosocial and medical history. Most agencies have generic templates of intake questions that could be completed between 30 minutes to 45 minutes. A well-done intake will reveal a lot about the client's source of anguish, an idea on the severity and most likely a guideline for the assessment and diagnosis stage.

A responsive intake specialist should be sure that the intake is conducted in peaceful environment- normal room temperature, some privacy, less traffic area, and client friendly wall ornaments, decoration and paint. It has been observed that these conditions or the lack of, can contribute to overall outcome of the intake process. I postulate that the relationship building stage will be exhausted within the first and second sessions of contracted meetings.

Intake Form Sample

Exquisite Delight Counseling
Daytona Beach, Florida. 32114

Service Date:

| **DSM V** | *(Date of Face-to-Face)* | **Start Time:** | **Stop Time:** |

(Treatment plan needs to be completed within 14 days of the date of the intake. The assessment or psychosocial evaluation is an integral part of a productive counseling progress.)

I.   PRESENTING PROBLEM *(reason why individual is seeking services)*

Past Psychiatric/Psychological History: *(including past medications)*

Current Medications, including psychotropic, over-the-counter, herbal remedies *(include all meds taken over past 6 months)*				
Current Medications	**Dosage**	**Frequency**	**Prescribed By**	**Reason for prescription**

Allergies:

Past medical history (include hospitalizations, surgeries, physical limitations):

Family/social history (including minor children, associated needs and risk factors):

Current and past employment history (include past trainings):

Education (include highest grade completed, schools attended, special education, discipline problems, etc.):

Current Legal _____ **No legal involvement**

II.   DRUG/ALCOHOL USE HISTORY

SUBSTANCE USE HISTORY

(Include experimentation & accidental ingestion. Include alcohol, tobacco, and caffeine)

Drug	Method	Age 1st used	Age last used	Onset of heavy use	# days used in last 30	Amount used in last 48 hrs.	1st as RX?	Last used when?	Amount used daily/weekly	Drug of choice

Is individual compliant with medications?   Yes   No   If no, please explain:
_____ _____

Allergies:

Past medical history (include hospitalizations, surgeries, physical abilities):

Family/social history (children, siblings, and risk factors):

Current and past employment history (include volunteer and internship):

Education (include highest grade completed, schools attended, and special training, etc.):

Current Legal Status: ___ No legal involvement

Pending Charges	Probation	Jail Time	Parole	No Record
__	__	__	__	______

III. Psycho Social History *(Describe Social Impressions under each category.)*

Appearance

__ Well groomed

__ Disheveled

__ Bizarre

__ Other:

Describe:

Mood

__ Normal   __ Euphoric

__ Depressed   __ Irritable

__ Anxious   __ Other:

Describe:

Affect

__ Appropriate   __ Inappropriate

Thought Content

__ Normal   __ Paranoid

Code	DSM V __	**Specify**	**Mild**	**Moderate**	**Severe**
Code	___ __	_______			
Code	___ __	_______			
Code	___ __	_______			
Code	___ __	_______			
Code	___ __	_______			
Code	___ __	_______			
Code	___ __	_______			
Code	___ __				

___ Sad   ___ Angry   ___ Morbid   ___ Phobias

___ Flat   ___ Constricted   ___ Somatic Complaints   ___ Obsessive

___ Anxious   ___ Labile   ___ Aggressive

___ Other: ___ Other:

Describe: Describe:

IV. DIAGNOSTIC INFORMATION *(codes & nomenclature)*

_______________________   _______________________
Client Signature   Intake Specialist Signature

_______________________   _______________________

       Date   Date

Stage 2. Assessment and Diagnosis

Upon completion of the Intake form, the next step is to use the information from the intake to design a psychosocial evaluation or mental health summary. This is a written assessment summary that describes client's response and invariably used to determine possible diagnosis and the best treatment plan. This is also the stage when counselor/client relationship becomes solid and planted on concrete grounds.

This is a coordination phase with the client to establish the level of severity-mild, moderate, or severe; thus, leading to a determined mode of treatment- either as an in-resident patient or outpatient, length of therapy, number of sessions, and the milieu of choice. Diagnostic Statistic Manual V guidelines is specific to how to determine diagnostic suggestions that is based on the level of severity of either mild, moderate, or severe codes. It is of paramount importance to coordinate with the Intake Specialist and to within an abbreviated time transform the impressions from the intake to a sensible Psychosocial Evaluation Summary.

Sample of Psychosocial Evaluation Summary

Psychosocial/Mental Health Evaluation Summary

Name: Carol Black

Date of Birth: September 20, 1981

Date of Evaluation: December 8, 2017

Age: 36

Reason for Referral

Ms. Black is a 36-year-old Black female who was referred for a psychological evaluation by Project Warm Center. She was admitted into a Residential program on 04/27/2017 and, was discharged after a 90-day in residence rehab. Prior to living at home, she was in detox for five days. She stated that her aunt court-ordered her to treatment in the early part of April.

Mental Health Physical History

She stated she was hospitalized at Northwell Health at the age of 17 or 18. She was vague about the exact reasons for this hospitalization but evidently her parents felt she was acting erratic and refused to go to her part-time restaurant job. She states she has high blood pressure, bronchitis and high cholesterol. She is taking medication for her blood pressure, but she could not remember the exact name of the medication. She is also taking another medication, possibly for her asthma.

Family History

Her natural parents were married but her father left when she was two or three years of age. Her maternal grandmother evidently cared for her after her father left. She last saw her father in 1985 and knows very little about him. She did, however, state that he drank but she does not know to what extent he had a problem with alcohol use. Her mother died during childbirth at the age of 29. She has one brother, aged 38, and two sisters, ages 41 and 43. Her 41-year-old sister reportedly had a drug and/or alcohol problem at one point in her life.

Abuse History

Ms. Black stated that she experienced emotional and physical abuse from her boyfriend she met while she was in the 11th grade (high school) who started to physically abuse her three years after they moved in together. She stated that she did not leave the relationship because her twin girls and that she is afraid to start all over alone or move in with another man who is not the biological father to her girls.

Substance Abuse History

She began drinking at the age of 15 or 16. She would drink anywhere from one-half pint to a-six pack- prior to 1996 but, after her boyfriend went to prison for 5 years, she began to drink more than three six packs daily. She denies ever having any blackouts or DT's. She also denies ever using any other drugs. This is reportedly her first treatment experience and she plan to attend AA meeting as part of her treatment plan. When asked if she felt like she has an alcohol problem she said. "I kind of think I do."

Educational/Occupational History

She dropped out of school during the 12th grade and never obtained her GED. She has worked at motels and she last had a steady job in January of 2014. Ms. Black stated that she receives financial support from her aunt after her employment benefit ran out.

Marital History

She is unmarried but leave at the same house she has been leaving before her boyfriend went to prison. She has two children-twin girls for the boyfriend who promised to treat her better after returning from prison.

Criminal Justice System History

She was arrested for driving while under the influence in 2007 and was ordered to complete a 30-day community service for the arrest.

Mental Status Findings

Mood and Affect:	There was an indication of suppressed sadness episode with moments and some anxious mood elation. Her affect seems to be appropriate with no indication of blunting, flatness or liable.
Quality of Thinking:	There was no indication of circumstantial or tangential thinking. She was able to relate her history in a rational, sequential and coherent fashion.
Concentration:	She could count backward from 20 to 1 in seconds without error. She could say her ABC's in 7 seconds without error. She could count forward by threes from 1 to 45 in 35 seconds with two errors.
Orientation to Time, Place and Person:	She was oriented as to time, place and person.
Memory Recent and Remote:	She could recall 7 digits forward and 3 digits backward. There is no evidence of difficulty with her remote memory.
Hallucinations and Perceptual Disturbances:	There was no indication of hallucinations or perceptual disturbances.

Behavior During Evaluation

During her evaluation, Ms. Black was very outspoken but cooperative. However, she seems to be somewhat guarded and evasive when discussing her past alcohol use history. She was also somewhat ambivalent in deciding the first time she noticed a sad moment that lasted more than a week. She had little interest in a 12-step recovery program and seemed only minimally motivated for treatment. There were no behavioral indications of anxiety, depression or thought disorder.

Results

Individuals with this pattern are often tense, anxious, hostile and irritable. They are usually described as being emotionally labile, restless, hyperactive, indecisive, and emotionally inappropriate. Other descriptions include disoriented, obsessional, suspicious, ambivalent, vague, demanding, and over talkative. They are likely to remain socially isolated and to have poor social relationships, especially with the opposite sex. Sexual conflicts and problems are common.

The thinking of many of those with this profile is confused and unusual. Difficulty in concentration and problems with reality testing are common. They may evidence grandiosity, stereotyped thinking, feelings of perplexity, paranoia and other delusions or even hallucinations.

It should be noted that her MacAndrew Alcoholism Scale was highly elevated with a T-Score of 92. This is a much higher elevation than what is normally seen in women who are going through treatment for the first time. DSM V and ICD-10 codes were used for specific symptoms criterion diagnosis in substance induced anxiety and to endorse items indicating significant psychopathology.

From a personality point of view, she describes a constant and confusing undercurrent of tension, sadness and anger; She seems to be bothered and distracted by disruptive inner thoughts. She has an alienated self-image and describes life as one of social isolation and rejection. She over-interprets innocuous behavior as a sign of ridicule and humiliation.

She has a labile affect and is frequently irritable and displays erratic moodiness. She reports being easily frustrated and explosive. She feels misunderstood, unappreciated and demeaned by others. She seems to be characteristically pessimistic, disgruntled and disillusioned with life. She expresses a fear of losing independence and the power of self-determination. She is resistant to sources of external influence and control. She distorts events into personally logical but essentially irrational beliefs. She construes incidental events as critical of herself and seems to magnify minor and personally related intentions into proofs of purposeful deception and malice.

Clinical Scales indicate the distinct possibility of delusional thinking and may, at times, appear to be overtly psychotic. However, there was no evidence of psychosis during the interview portion of her evaluation. Her Drug and Alcohol Abuse Scales were both highly elevated. She also reported moderate levels of anxiety and depression.

Recommendations

(1)   Ms. Black overall psychological profile resembles either an individual who has been diagnosed as manic depressive or someone with co-dependency and trust issues. It is felt that her profile for a female who primarily use alcohol and other substance for recreation and amusement. As a result, a psychiatric evaluation is being recommended for consideration of medication, Medication should be given very cautiously as she may be very prone to relapse.

(2)   It is recommended that Ms. Black stay in a half-way residential treatment provided she can take her twin girls for a 90-day period. She may be somewhat resistant to doing this but, because of her overall thought processes and a moderate anxiety and depression level, this would insure her stability at least for the short term.

(3)   Ms. Black progress needs to be monitored very carefully. She should continue to participate in 12-step meetings and have urinalysis/breathalyzer tests randomly. At this point, it is extremely difficult to tell whether a co-occurring diagnosis is appropriate or whether Ms. Black is simply continuing to suffer from the effects of her prolonged substance use. A careful assessment while in treatment will help to make this distinction.

Diagnosis: 305.00(F10.10) Alcohol Use Disorder

                     311(F32.8) Unspecified Depressive Disorder

                     300.02(F41.1) Generalized Anxiety Disorder

Stage 3. Formulation and Setting Goals

This is the stage of interpretation of the impression gathered from the psychosocial evaluation summary. This information is then transferred to a treatment plan. The plan is an objective covered document with a focus on problems, goals, activities, accountability and the time frame for treatment completion. This formulation and goal setting stage should center around the time of the third session just for our purpose of articulation.

A treatment plan meeting is coordinated with other professionals like the nurse, psychologist, counselor, and the intake specialist within the milieu to create short term and long-term goals and to maintain objectives, activities, and accountability as needed for recovery time frame. Once the treatment plan meeting is formulated, the assigned counselor will seat with the client, to go over the plan and explain the process, and possible ways to accomplish what is agreed upon.

At the commencement of the process, the client may not understand details of the plan, but the counselor should be proactive about client's anticipation. If there is any disagreement, the counselor will take it to advisement and make minor changes in the process, it is then, the client can sign the treatment plan as presented. Counseling is an inclusive process because clients are entitled to participate in their own treatment. Therefore, for clients to sign the treatment plan is a mark of active participation that seem to ease the treatment journey.

Your expertise as a counselor tells you not to sweat little stuff; so, when clients fret about the process, it's your job to enlighten and bring clients along the path of success. One last thing, on this issue, avoid assuring clients that they will be well upon participation, by the same token, it is alright to promote the idea that you will do your best as a professional to work with them (clients) to the termination stage without predicting any indicated outcome of the relationship.

Simply put, avoid balking or setting yourself up for a failure; remember that clients need help due to confirmed state of incongruency and some unknown predicaments that impact progress, hence, they seek resolve for their issues. Some clients progress may be faster than that of others and that is natural without being bombastic or melodramatic about it.

Treatment Plan Template

Client Name: _____________________   Date:_______________

Counselor Name: _______________   Date:_______________

Problems	Goals	Objective	Activities	Accountability	Time Frame	Date Complete

_____________________   _____________________

Client Signature   Counselor Signature

_____________________   _____________________

Date   Date

Stage 4. Intervention and Problem Solving

This is the stage when all fundamentals and preparations culminate to the progress and or recovery as anticipated. The counselor in conjunction with the client considers the psychosocial summary as translated from the intake form, examines and evaluate the severity of issues, articulate the best recovery methodology and determine number of sessions, and coordinate goals to aid the recovery progress. As you have acquiesced, we imagine a contract of eight sessions for the practicality of our discussion for this book. Therefore, the intervention and problem-solving phase would be in the parameters of the fourth, fifth and sixth sessions.

By now, you have studied the parameters of client issues and discovered needs to assist you in moving the clients toward progress. For example, if you and the client have resolved and agreed to say eight weeks of problem solving sessions; you should make sure that the physical environment is appropriate for counseling and expressive sessions. Be double sure that your phone and your client's phone are mute, you need to set up comfortable chairs to reduce apprehension on both sides, you need to create a warm and inviting atmosphere, prepare the room with adequate lighting, and more importantly, the room should be safe from frequent interruptions. With all said, and done, a spigot light at the end of the tunnel is now lit and a reason to take the first step to reconciliation of sort in client's issue has emerged.

On the first session, the counselor should begin with warm greetings and allow for client's complete self-reintroduction. As you and the client build rapport, your horizon is widened, and your client becomes more receptive to questions because they are relaxed and ready for help

(Murphy & Dillion (2008). As you can imagine, there is no better time than the moment of an

incandescent light; this is the appropriate time towards the end of the first session to introduce a

consent form-the form covers details about the counseling process, the counseling experience,

confidentiality, missed appointments, questions and concerns and permission for recording or

sharing information that could help clients progress. (See Consent Form Sample below)

Counseling Informed Consent Form Sample

Exquisite Delight Counseling
Daytona Beach, Florida. 32114

Informed Consent Statement

Counseling is a relationship that works in part because of clearly defined rights and responsibilities held by each person. As a client in a counseling relationship, you have certain rights that are important for you to know about because this is your therapy, whose goal is your well-being. There are also certain limitations to those rights that you should be aware of. As a therapist, I have corresponding responsibilities to you, too.

My Responsibilities to You as Your Counselor

I. Confidentiality

According to American Disability Act of 1990, you have the absolute right to the confidentiality of your therapy. I cannot and will not tell anyone else what you have told me, or even that you are in therapy with me without your prior written permission. Under the provisions of the Health Care Information Act of 1992, I may legally speak to another health care provider or a member of your family about you without your prior consent, but I will not do so unless the situation is an emergency. I will always protect your privacy considering the public good as the overriding factor, even if you do release me in writing to share information about you. You may direct me to share information with whomever you chose, and you can change your mind and revoke that permission at any time. You may request anyone you wish to attend a therapy session with you. You are also protected under the provisions of the Federal Health Insurance Portability and Accountability Act (HIPAA).

The following are legal exceptions to your right to confidentiality. I would inform you of any time when I think I will have to put these into effect.

1. If I have good reason to believe that you will harm another person, I must attempt to inform that person and warn them of your intentions. I must also contact the police and ask them to protect your intended victim.

2. If I have good reason to believe that you are abusing or neglecting a child or vulnerable adult, or if you give me information about someone else who is doing this, I must inform Child Protective Services within 48 hours and Adult Protective Services immediately.
3. If I believe that you are in imminent danger of harming yourself, I may legally break confidentiality and call the police or the county crisis team. I am not obligated to do this, and would explore all other options with you before I took this step. If at that point you were unwilling to take steps to guarantee your safety, I would call the crisis team.
4. Do not tell me anything you wish you kept secret unless it is required by the court, or required for public safety reasons.

II. Record-keeping

I keep brief records of each session noting the dates we meet, the topics we cover, progress reports from the client's perspective, interventions and impressions from the therapist and next steps. My records are kept private and not shared with others, in accordance with HIPPA requirements.

III. Diagnosis

In my practice, I use DSM V: I also work diligently to accommodate your concerns about insurance related form of payment, I will give out any information about you that has nothing to do with your progress for recovery. Diagnoses are technical terms that describe the nature of your problems and something about whether they are short-term or long-term problems. If I do use a diagnosis, I will discuss it with you.

IV. Other Rights

You have the right to ask questions about anything that happens in therapy. You have the right to refuse any form of therapy that seem to infringe on your cultural and or religious belief I'm always willing to discuss how and why I've decided to do what I'm doing, and to look at alternatives that might work better. You should feel free to ask me to try a contemporary approach that you think will be helpful. You can ask me about my training for working with your concerns, and can request that I refer you to someone else if you decide I'm not the right counselor for you. You are free to leave therapy at any time.

If you believe you will need a counselor with 24-hour coverage I will be happy to make a referral. You should call 911 or go to the nearest hospital emergency room rather than waiting for me to call you back. If I am out of town for an unexpected length of time, I will give you the name of a colleague you can contact in case of an urgent need.

Fees

As of 1/1/18: Individual therapy or couples therapy is $75 per 45-50 minutes session. You will be asked to pay for each session at the time of the session. Payment can be by, cash, or credit card. An email statement of the month's sessions will be furnished to you at the end of each session with attachments about the next session. You can use the statement for tax purposes or for reimbursement.

Note from Dr. Oludare O Eniwaye:

I use art therapy and dog companion approach for clients who are animal friendly. If you no longer feel that I am the best or right practitioner for you, I will offer referrals to other sources of care, without any regret or malice.

My Training and Approach to Therapy

I have a Ph.D. in Human Services earned in 2005 at Capella University, Minneapolis, MN. I am a Human Services Board-Certified Practitioner (HS-BCP). My areas of special training and expertise include: addictions counseling, developmental disability care, aging, TBI, dementia, neurocognitive management and the use of life coach model and approach.

I may suggest that you get involved in additional or adjunctive forms of support, such as additional counseling or a support group as part of your work with me. If another health care person is working with you, I may request a release of information from you so that I can communicate freely with that person about your care.

I am away from the office several times in the year for extended vacations or to attend professional meetings. If I am not taking and responding to phone messages during those times I will have someone cover my practice. I will tell you well in advance of any anticipated lengthy absences.

Your Responsibilities as a Therapy Client
A typical Session last for 45-50 minutes. If you are going to be late or need to cancel the session, be sure to give me a (24) hours in advance so that we can reschedule with you within the same calendar week.

____

Client's Signature/Date   Counselor's Signature/Date

Stage 5. Termination and After Care

At the beginning of this discussion we talked about types of relationships; the counselor/client alliance is not a never-ending relationship; the enduring work though is a work collaboration that is well-defined at this stage and, this is not a sad thing. In fact, both parties should be looking forward to it. Yes, you might be losing a client but, no one is a loser. Some people have asked me; how do I know when to plan for termination? To that, I say, you should start planning for this stage right from the first session but, more importantly, if you have scheduled eight-sessions in your contract with the client, the seventh session is the bridge to cross and it is philosophically appropriate to start questions dealing with terminating the relationship and replacing with aftercare agenda.

Obviously, if you and your client have successfully reached the seventh session out of the imaginary eight sessions, the progress is well-manifested, otherwise you would have reached an unspoken termination way-back during stage three which might have corresponded with the third or the forth session. So, during the seventh session, you want to go over the progress both of you have witnessed, it is also advantageous to touch on goals that have been graded and achieved to maximize the potential of success and what could be done differently.

By the time you get to the Eight session, you can count your accolades and virtually pat each other on the back, as it were. Now is the time to talk about what now; questions, suggestions, and plans for the aftercare. Anticipate that your client is probably massaging a separation anxiety fumes that are yet verbally expressed. You could ask point view questions like, what is your thinking about the process so far? Or where do you see yourself three months from now? These or

similar question clear the air and create space for a workable aftercare.

Towards the middle of the eighth counseling session, you should lay out a concrete plan for

an aftercare that follows the client well into about ninety days after the last contracted meeting. As

far as I am concerned, the mark of a true counselor is revealed in his effort to endorse a good

aftercare. The Aftercare could be linked to group sessions or could be individualized to monitor

relapse ideations, job skills, and relationship skills. It has been observed that aftercare plan done

with succinctness reduces the rate of recidivism by fifty-percent (Arbour, Hambley, & Ho.,2011).

What's Next

We have come to the part of the journey where as your Guide, the ball is now in you court, and I want you to decide how to use the information in this hand-book to benefit you and your clients. After over fifteen years in the helping profession, I have observed, listened and learned some things that may be beneficial to me and you in this profession. Thus, my approach to this writing may be a little unorthodox, but I wanted to write with less technicality so that this information could be readily available and digested by those who just need basic problem-solving knowhow on these issues. Also, I am aware of the consummate helping professionals out there with jingoistic ideology, remember that knowledge improves opportunity.

There may be more than eight huddles of thought process ruminating in the abused victim's mind; these make your job as a counselor more difficult if you are not asking the right questions, but, the door is now opened to expand your knowledge base. This is not the panacea of see all solve all, but we can move forward with one accord and in unity to help clients in our care.

Handbook Exercise

1. A. Write a 2-page account about your childhood memory concerning views about family relationships, divorce, religious beliefs, attitude toward strangers, culture, abuse, and work ethics. B. How has this impacted who you are today as a member of the society in general? After writing with authenticity, find an audience, read your account aloud to them: You will take a load off your heart: Self -Therapy.

2. Explain in your own words the role of recreational drugs and alcohol in the prevalence of comorbid dysfunctions.

3. What qualities define a good counselor and how can you demonstrate these attributes.

4. Who is your role model and what attributes of this person you would absolutely share with the world?

5. Design a Self-Help Mantra on a specific addiction or a self-deprecating habit.

6. Create a Counseling Plan using holistic approach for a make-belief client.

7. Design and create a 20-30 pages Counseling Agency Handbook for your counseling practice using the Publisher Program. (Use as many as possible content outlines from the handbook content samples below).

8. Explain types of questions used in the counseling process and the significance of these methods.

9. Explain what you will do to resolve issues with a difficult, resistant or uncooperative client.

10. Print out a code of ethics guide from an Organization you belong to, or the one you want to be part of.

Employee Handbook Sample
TABLE OF CONTENTS

Welcome To
Exquisite Delight Counseling Agency

The Agency has prepared this handbook to provide you with an overview of the Organization policies, benefits, and rules. It is intended to familiarize you with essential information about the company, as well as provide guidelines for your employment experience with us to foster a safe and healthy work environment. Please understand that this booklet only highlights agency policies, practices, and benefits for your personal understanding and cannot, therefore, be construed as a legal document. It is intended to provide general information about the policies, benefits, and regulations governing the employees of the company, and is not intended to be an express or implied contract. The guidelines presented in this handbook are not intended to be a substitute for sound management, judgment, and discretion.

It is obviously not possible to anticipate every situation that may arise in the workplace or to provide information that answers every possible question. In addition, circumstances will undoubtedly require that policies, practices, and benefits described in this handbook change from time to time. Accordingly, the company reserves the right to modify, supplement, rescind, or revise any provision of this handbook from time to time as it deems necessary or appropriate in its sole discretion with or without notice to you.

No organization is free from day-to-day problems, but we believe our policies and practices will help resolve such problems. All of us must work together to make the agency a viable, healthy, and organization. This is the only way we can provide a satisfied and congruent clients e that promotes genuine environment of trust and stability. If any statements in this handbook are not clear to you, please contact the agency CEO or his designated representative for clarification. This handbook supersedes all prior policies, procedures, and handbooks of the agency.

PHILOSOPHY OF THE ORGANIZATION

OPEN-DOOR POLICY

In keeping with the agency's philosophy of open communication, all employees, staff and counselors have the right and are encouraged to speak freely with the CEO about counselor/client related concerns only if this will do no harm to the client.

We urge you to go directly to your supervisor to discuss ideas to enhance improvements, recommendations, concerns and other issues of importance. If, after talking with your supervisor, you feel the need for additional discussion, you are encouraged to speak with the CEO.

The most important relationship you will develop at the agency will be between you and the senior counselor. However, should you need support from someone other than your supervisor, the entire management team, including the CEO, is committed to resolving your individual concerns in a timely and appropriate manner.

EQUAL EMPLOYMENT OPPORTUNITY

It is the policy of the Agency to provide equal employment opportunity to all employees and applicants for employment and not to discriminate on any basis prohibited by law, including race, color, sex, age, religion, national origin, disability, marital status or veteran status. It is our intent and desire that equal employment opportunities will be provided in employment, recruitment, selection, compensation, benefits, promotion, demotion, layoff, termination and all other terms and conditions of employment. The CEO and all managerial personnel are committed to this policy and its enforcement.

Staff and Counselors are directed to bring any violation of this policy to the immediate attention of their supervisor or the CEO. Any staff who violates this policy or knowingly retaliates against other staff reporting or complaining of a violation of this policy shall be subject to immediate disciplinary action, up to and including discharge. Complaints brought under this policy will be promptly investigated and handled with due regard for the privacy and respect of all involved.

HARASSMENT POLICY

The Agency will not tolerate harassment or intimidation of our employees on any basis prohibited by law, including race, color, sex, age, religion, national origin, handicap, disability, marital status, or veteran status. Moreover, any suggestions made to any employee that sexual favors will affect any term or condition of employment with the agency will not be tolerated. It is the policy of the Agency that any harassment, including acts creating a hostile work environment or any other discriminatory acts directed against our employees, will result in discipline, up to and including discharge. The Agency also will not tolerate any such harassment of our employees by our clients or vendors.

For purposes of this policy, sexual harassment is defined as any type of sexually-oriented conduct, whether intentional or not, that is unwelcome and has the purpose or effect of creating a work environment that is hostile, offensive or coercive. The following are examples of conduct that, depending upon the circumstances, may constitute sexual harassment:

- Unwelcome sexual jokes, language, epithets, advances or propositions;
- Written or oral abuse of a sexual nature, sexually degrading or vulgar words to describe an individual;
- The display of sexually suggestive objects, pictures, posters or cartoons;
- Unwelcome comments about an individual's body;
- Asking questions about sexual conduct;
- Unwelcome touching, leering, whistling, brushing against the body, or suggestive, insulting or obscene comments or gestures;
- Demanding sexual favors in exchange for favorable reviews, assignments, promotions, or continued employment, or promises of the same.

Employees must bring any violation of this policy to the immediate attention of their supervisor or the Agency. The Agency will thoroughly investigate all such claims with due regard for the privacy of the individuals involved. Any staff who knowingly retaliates against a staff who has reported workplace harassment or discrimination shall be subject to immediate disciplinary action, up to and including discharge.

WORKING AND COMPENSATION

EMPLOYMENT ON AN AT-WILL BASIS

All staff of the agency, regardless of their classification or position, are employed on an at-will basis. This means that each employee's employment is terminable at the will of the employee or the company at any time, with or without cause and with or without notice. No officer, agent, representative, or employee of the agency has any authority to enter into any agreement with any employee or applicant for employment on other than on an at-will basis. Furthermore, nothing contained in the policies, procedures, handbooks, manuals, job descriptions, application for employment, or any other document of the company shall in any way create an express or implied contract of employment or an employment relationship on other than an at-will basis.

ATTENDANCE AND REPORTING TO WORK

Each staff is important to the overall success of our clients. People skill is our bottom line, when you are not present, someone else must attend to your clients. Consequently, you are expected to keep your scheduled appointments. Reporting to work on time means that you are ready to take care of your clients, and that boost the trust within the agency.

The agency depends on its counselors to be people of their words always and manage their schedules promptly. Excessive absenteeism and/or tardiness will lead to disciplinary action, up to and including termination. The determination of excessive absenteeism will be made at the discretion of the agency. Absence from work for three consecutive days without properly notifying your supervisor will be considered a voluntary resignation. After two days' absence, you may be required to provide documentation from your physician to support an injury- or illness-related absence, and to ensure that you may safely return to work.

If you expect to be absent from the job for an approved reason (e.g., paid time off or a leave of absence), you should notify your supervisor of your upcoming absence as far in advance as possible. If you unexpectedly need to be absent from or late to work, you must notify your supervisor prior to the start of your scheduled workday that you will be late or absent and provide the reason for that absence or tardiness. If your supervisor is not available, you should contact the agency's central office prior to the start of your scheduled workday. Leave your number so that your supervisor can return your call. Failure to properly contact us will result in an unexcused absence for disciplinary purposes. Your attendance record is a part of your overall performance rating. Your attendance may be included during your review and may be considered for other disciplinary action up to and including termination.

Where possible, medical and dental appointments should be scheduled around your assigned work hours; otherwise, they may be considered absences without pay. If you are unable to schedule an appointment before or after your shift, you are required to talk to your supervisor to make special arrangements.

WORKDAY HOURS AND SCHEDULING

The regularly scheduled workday for our office is: Monday through Friday, 7:30-8:00 a.m. to 4:30-5:00 p.m. The usual expected workday at jobsites is 8:00 a.m. to 4:30 p.m. These start and end times are only guidelines, however, and employees are required to be present for work during the workday established for them by their supervisors or by the company president.

Particularly at jobsites, this regular schedule may vary depending on such factors as weather, materials supply, permit approval, etc. If you are unsure about expected starting times on any job assignment, ask your supervisor for clarification.

In case of unplanned conditions, such as severe weather, that may force a schedule change at the last minute, you should contact your supervisor or call the office directly.

The agency does not generally schedule rest periods or breaks, other than meal breaks, during the workday. However, if the company does schedule such rest periods or breaks, they will be paid breaks and will usually be for 15 minutes. For lunch or meals, our policy is:

- Field employee meals will be 30 minutes.

- Office employee meals will be 1 hour.
- The meal period is unpaid.
- All employees are required to take a lunch break and no employee is authorized, without prior supervisory approval, to perform work during the lunch period.

RECORDING HOURS WORKED

All hourly employees are required to keep a time sheet. On your time sheet, you must correctly record the job number, job code, and time spent on each job number or code for each day worked. The agency will provide you with a time sheet for reporting your hours. Only you are authorized to record your own time.

Completed time sheets are due in the office no later than 8:00 a.m. on the Wednesday following the end of a pay period. Failure to turn in time sheets by this deadline may delay your paycheck for that week.

PAY PERIOD AND PAYDAY

The Agency issues paychecks each Friday, on a weekly basis. Pay periods start on Wednesday morning and end on Tuesday afternoon. Therefore, each Friday, you will receive a paycheck for all hours worked in the pay period ending the previous Tuesday afternoon. If an employee uses direct deposit, the employee's pay may not be available for withdrawal from his or her bank account until the following Monday.

WORKWEEK & OVERTIME

The Agency's workweek begins on Wednesday at 12:01 a.m. and ends on Tuesday at 12:00 midnight.

Occasionally it may be necessary for an employee to work beyond his or her normal workday hours. Overtime pay is paid only when work is scheduled, approved, and made known to you in advance by your supervisor. Under no circumstances shall an employee work overtime without the prior approval of his or her supervisor.

Hourly employees will receive overtime pay at a rate of one-and-one-half times their regular hourly rate for all hours worked more than 40hrs in a workweek.

To the extent possible, overtime will be distributed equally among all employees in the same classification and position, provided that the employees concerned are equally capable of performing the available work. Decisions regarding overtime work will be made by the Production Coordinator or his/her representative. Any staff asked to work overtime will be expected to rearrange his/her personal schedule to work the requested overtime.

<u>**HOLIDAYS**</u>

The agency observes the following holidays:

- New Year's Day
- Memorial Day
- Fourth of July
- Labor Day
- Thanksgiving
- Christmas

Full-time employees will be paid for these holidays provided the employee was present for work on the workdays immediately before and after that holiday, or had an acceptable excuse for being absent on any such days. If a paid holiday falls within an employee's vacation period, the holiday will not be counted as a vacation day.

Part-time staff are not eligible for holiday pay.

<u>**EMPLOYMENT CLASSIFICATIONS**</u>

Upon being hired by the Agency, all new counselors/employees must serve a ninety (90) calendar day introductory period. It is especially important that you make your supervisor aware of any questions or problems you may encounter during this period. Your performance will be carefully monitored during this period. At the end of the introductory period, your performance will be reviewed, and if it has been satisfactory, you will become a Regular Full-Time or Regular Part-Time Employee. Satisfactory completion of the introductory period does not entitle you to employment for any specific term, but does entitle you to participation in many of the Agency's employee benefits programs.

For the sole purpose of determining the allowance of certain employee benefits, employees are classified as:

1. <u>Regular Full-Time Employees</u> - An employee who has satisfactorily completed the introductory period and is scheduled to work an average of forty (40) hours per week on a regular and continuous basis.

2. <u>Regular Part-Time Employees</u> - An employee who has satisfactorily completed the introductory period and is usually scheduled to work less than an average of forty (40) hours per week but not less than ten (10) hours per week on a regular and continuous basis.

3. <u>Temporary Employees</u> - An employee whose services are anticipated to be of limited duration falls into this classification. Temporary employees are not eligible

for participation in those employee benefits programs made available for the Agency Regular Full-Time and Regular Part-Time Employees, although separate benefit plans may be available for certain temporary employees assigned to work at the Agency. Any such employees will be separately notified of any such programs. Service as a temporary does not count as service as a Regular Employee for benefit eligibility purposes.

For payroll purposes, employees will be classified as one of the following:

1. <u>Exempt Employees</u> - Certain employees such as executive, administrative, professional and counselors paid on a salary basis for all hours worked each week. Certain professionals may also be exempt, regardless of whether they are paid on a salary or hourly basis. These professionals are expected to work whatever hours are required to accomplish their duties, even if it exceeds their normal workweek. No overtime premium pay will be paid to exempt employees in most circumstances.

2. <u>Non-Exempt Employees</u> - All employees who are not identified as exempt employees are considered non-exempt employees. Non-exempt employees are eligible for payment of overtime premium pay.

MAINTAINING YOUR PERSONNEL RECORDS

It is your responsibility to provide current information regarding your address, telephone number, insurance beneficiaries, change in dependents, marital status, etc. Please use the personnel records form to note any changes in your address, phone number, emergency contact information, marital status, number of dependents, etc. Changes in exemptions for tax purposes will only be made upon the receipt of a completed W-4 form.

PERSONNEL FILES

Personnel files are the property of the agency, and do not belong to the employee. However, upon request, the agency will provide employees with copies of performance evaluations and other performance-related documents that the employee has previously received.

PERFORMANCE EVALUATIONS

Staff and other professionals may have their job performance reviewed on an annual basis by either their supervisor or by the CEO of the agency.

STANDARDS AND EXPECTATIONS FOR THE WORKPLACE

SAFETY

The agency believes in maintaining safe and healthy working conditions for our employees. However, to achieve our goal of providing a safe workplace, each employee must be safety conscious. We have established the following policies and procedures that allow us to provide safe and healthy working conditions. We expect each employee to follow these policies and procedures, to act safely, and to report unsafe conditions to his or her supervisor in a timely manner.

Reporting Unethical Situations or Practices

Counselors and other professionals are expected to continually be on the lookout for client rights, privacy and safe practices. If you observe unethical situations, you should consult with the individual, if possible, and report that situation to your supervisor immediately. If you have a question regarding ethical guidelines and acceptable practices, ask your supervisor for clarification.

If you observe a coworker using an unsafe practice, you are expected to mention this to the coworker and to your supervisor. Likewise, if a coworker brings to your attention an unsafe practice you may be using, please thank the coworker and make any necessary adjustments to what you are doing. Safety at work is a team effort.

Maintaining a Safe Office

We expect employees to establish and maintain a safe worksite. This includes but is not limited to the following applications:

- Maintaining proper fall-protection systems.
- Building and maintaining walkways, handrails, and guardrails.
- Maintaining accessible sidewalk, ramps, and wheelchair trails
- Inspecting tools and equipment for defects before use.
- Keeping walkways clear of debris.
- Construction and use of safe scaffolding.
- Inspecting, cleaning, and properly storing tools and equipment after use.
- Following established safety rules.

Using Safety Equipment

Where needed, the company provides its employees with appropriate safety equipment and devices. You are required to use the equipment provided in the manner designated as proper and safe by the manufacturer. Failure to properly use safety equipment may lead to disciplinary action, up to and including termination.

If you require safety equipment that has not been provided, contact your supervisor before performing the job duty for which you need the safety equipment.

<u>Reporting an Injury</u>

Employees are required to report any injury, accident, or safety hazard immediately to their supervisor(s). Minor cuts or abrasions must be treated on the spot. More serious injuries or accidents will be treated accordingly. Serious injuries must be reported on the injury or accident report form available in the office.

<u>Hazard Communications</u>

If you believe that you are dealing with a hazardous material and lack the appropriate information and/or safety equipment, contact your supervisor immediately.

<u>CARE OF EQUIPMENT AND SUPPLIES</u>

All employees are expected to take care of all equipment and supplies provided to them. You are responsible for maintaining this material in proper working condition and for promptly reporting any unsafe or improper functioning of this material to your supervisor.

Neglect, theft, and/or destruction of the Agency's materials are grounds for disciplinary action, up to and including termination.

<u>SMOKING AT THE WORKPLACE</u>

The Agency's policy is to provide smoke-free environments for our employees, clients, and the public. Smoking of any kind is prohibited inside our office and on the road to clients. We have voted for a smoke free campus, therefore, no smoking within 150ft from our office. Employees who take excessive smoke breaks may be required to work longer hours to make up for time lost smoking.

Employees are also responsible to inform all those working on our job sites of this smoke-free policy, and report to their supervisor any violation of this policy.

<u>VIOLENCE AND WEAPONS</u>

The Agency believes in maintaining a safe and healthy workplace, in part by promoting open, friendly, and supportive working relationships among all employees. Violence or threats of violence have no place in our business. Violence is not an effective solution to any problem. Employees are strictly prohibited from bringing any weapons, including knives, pistols, rifles, stun guns, Mace, etc., to the worksite or office. Neither threats of violence nor fighting will be tolerated. Furthermore, if you have a problem that is creating stress or otherwise making you agitated, you are encouraged to discuss it with your supervisor.

You are expected to immediately report to your supervisor any violation of this policy. Any employee found threatening another employee, fighting, and/or carrying weapons to the worksite will be subject to disciplinary action, up to and including termination.

DRUG-FREE WORKPLACE

The Agency does not tolerate the presence of illegal drugs or the illegal use of legal drugs in our workplace. The use, possession, distribution, or sale of controlled substances such as drugs or alcohol, or being under the influence of such controlled substances is strictly prohibited while on duty, while on the company's premises or worksites, or while operating the company's equipment or vehicles. The use of illegal drugs as well as the illegal use of legal drugs is a threat to us all because it promotes problems with safety, customer service, productivity, and our ability to survive and prosper as a business. If you need to take a prescription drug that affects your ability to perform your job duties, you are required to discuss possible accommodations with your supervisor. Violation of this policy will result in disciplinary action, up to and including termination.

Prior to employment, each potential employee must undergo a drug test. The company may also require employees to take random drug tests during their employment with the company. A positive result on any such drug test is grounds for immediate termination.

Your receipt of this policy statement and signature on the handbook acknowledgment form signify your agreement to comply with this policy.

Any employee who is convicted of violating criminal drug statutes must notify an appropriate officer or senior official of the company of that conviction within five days of the conviction. Failure to do so may lead to disciplinary action.

RESPONDING TO CLIENTS INQUIRIES AND PROBLEMS

At the agency, client satisfaction is the measure of our success. It is the responsibility of each employee, within reason, to interact with the client to achieve this goal.

APPEARANCE AND DRESS

To present a business-like, professional image to our clients and the public, all employees are required to wear appropriate clothing on the job. By necessity, the dress standards for the office are somewhat different than for road trips and home visits.

- For the agency office, casual to business-style attire is appropriate. Employees should neatly groom and clothes should be clean and in good repair. Leisure clothes such as cut-offs or halter tops are not acceptable attire for the office. The agency will provide employees with shirts bearing the Agency's logo, which employees are expected to wear as appropriate in the business office.

- For jobsites, employees are expected to wear work clothes appropriate for work to be done. Employees should be sensitive to the location and context of their work and should be ready to adjust their dress if the circumstances so warrant. Employees at a jobsite should wear clothing that protects their safety dress shoes, covered toes no flip-flops) and wear clothing with professional outlook (e.g., shirts tucked in). The agency will provide employees with polo shirts bearing the Agency's logo, according to expected guidelines and as necessary.

CONFLICTS OF INTEREST

You should avoid external business, financial, or employment interests that conflict with the agency's business interests or with your ability to perform your job duties. This applies to your possible relationships with any other employer, consultant, contractor, customer, or supplier.

Violations of this rule may lead to disciplinary action, up to and including termination.

CODE OF ETHICAL CONDUCT

Exquisite Delight Counseling strictly abide by the code of ethics of American Counseling Association and the guidelines of American Disability Act. To avoid any appearance of a conflict of interest, counselors are expected to abide by the following code of ethical conduct. Please consult your supervisor or an official of the agency if you have any questions.

Employees of the agency should not solicit anything of value from any person or organization with whom the company has a current or potential business relationship.

Employees of the agency should not accept any item of value from any party in exchange for or relating to a business transaction between the company and that other party.

Employees may accept items of incidental value (generally, no more than $25) from clients, suppliers, or others if the gift is not given in response to solicitation on your part and if it implies no exchange for business purposes. Items may include gifts, gratuities, food, drink and entertainment.

If you are faced with and are unsure how to handle a situation that you believe has the potential to violate this code of ethical conduct, notify your supervisor or the company president.

Violations of this code may lead to disciplinary action, up to and including termination.

SOLICITATION AND DISTRIBUTION

For the safety, convenience, and protection of all employees, the company has adopted the following rules concerning solicitation and the distribution of materials:

- The agency prohibits solicitation and distribution of non-company materials on Company property or at Company jobsites always.

PERSONAL CALLS, VISITS, AND BUSINESS

The agency expects the full attention of its employees while they are working. Although employees may occasionally have to take care of personal matters during the workday, employees should try to conduct such personal business either before or after the workday or during breaks or meal periods. Regardless of when any personal call is made, it should be kept short.

Employees should also limit incoming personal calls, visits, or personal transactions. The agency phones should be available to serve the clients, and non-business use of the phones can hurt the company's business. A pattern of excessive personal phone calls, personal visits, and/or private/ business dealings is not acceptable and may lead to disciplinary action

BUSINESS EXPENSES

Employees may occasionally incur expenses on behalf of the agency. The agency will reimburse employees for typical business expenses, such as mileage (for example, when the agency asks an employee to travel to a different jobsite during the workday) and certain job-related supplies or materials. The agency will pay mileage reimbursements at the end of each month, upon receipt of the employee's mileage record. To be reimbursed for job-related supplies or materials, employees must deliver a receipt for the supplies or materials to the agency's business office within 7 days of the purchase. Employees may also turn in such receipts by attaching them to the employee's weekly time sheet for the week in which the employee made the purchase.

INSPECTION OF PERSONAL AND AGENCY'S PROPERTY

The agency's employees use the property and equipment the company owns and provides, and may also use the company's materials, information, and other supplies. While employees may decorate their office workspaces with their personal possessions (such as pictures, plants, and the like), employees must remember that property supplied by the agency remains the property of the company. The agency reserves the right to search any Agency property (e.g., personal computers, desks, lockers, or other storage areas) at any time. The agency also reserves the right to inspect private property (e.g., tool boxes, purses, briefcases) during the workday or as employees leave their worksites. Refusal to allow inspection may lead to disciplinary action, up to and including termination.

NETWORK AND ELECTRONIC RESOURCES POLICY

Network and Electronic Resources, such as computers, other hardware, software, e-mail, landline and cellular telephones, fax machines and internet access, are tools that the agency provides its employees to assist them in their work. These Network and Electronic Resources and related access systems are proprietary Agency property and subject to review or access by the Company at any time.

All employees who use the Agency's Network and Electronic Resources must follow the guidelines below:

1. Use Network and Electronic Resources for agency business purposes <u>only</u>.

2. Messages and communications sent via the Agency's Network and Electronic Resources are subject to subpoena and access by persons outside the agency and may be used in legal proceedings. Please consider this before sending any confidential messages or material via the Network and Electronic Resources.

3. E-Mail is not a substitute for face-to-face communication. If you have a conflict with someone it should be handled in person or over the telephone if a meeting is not possible.

4. Remember that all the Agency's policies, including but not limited to policies on Equal Employment Opportunity, Harassment, Confidentiality, Personal Conduct and Rules of Conduct, apply to the use of the Agency's Network and Electronic Resources. Employees must <u>not</u> review or forward sexually explicit, profane or otherwise unprofessional or unlawful material through the Agency's Network and Electronic Resources.

5. Passwords protecting the use of the Agency Network and Electronic Resources are the Agency's property and will be assigned to employees as needed. Employees may not change passwords without the consent of the company president. Employees must notify the CEO of all passwords and encryption keys assigned to or used by them, and must notify the CEO of any changes to such passwords or encryption keys.

6. Do not install any software or program on any agency's computer or other hardware without the express consent of your supervisor or the CEO.

7. The agency expressly prohibits the unauthorized use, installation, copying or distribution of copyrighted, trademarked or patented material.

8. Employees must not attempt to override or evade any program or measure installed by the Agency to protect the security or limit the use of its Network and Electronic Resources.

The Agency retains the right to review all communications conducted and data saved, reviewed or accessed via the Agency's Network and Electronic Resources, including Agency computers, e-mail and internet access. The agency does not permit its non-management employees to access or use any Agency password, e-mail or internet access other than their own. Inappropriate use of Network and Electronic Resources may result in discipline, up to and including discharge. Employees should be careful to safeguard their passwords, log off their terminals when not in use and not permit others to access Agency systems.

CONFIDENTIAL AND PROPRIETARY INFORMATION

The Agency considers its confidential and proprietary information, including the confidential and proprietary information of our customers, to be one of its most valuable assets. As a result, employees must carefully protect and must not disclose to any third party all confidential and proprietary information belonging to the Agency or its clients. Such protected information includes, but is not limited to, the following: matters of a technical nature, such as computer software, product sources, product research and designs; and matters of a business nature, such as customer lists, customer contact information, associate information, on-site program and support materials, candidate and recruit lists and information, personnel information, placement information, pricing lists, training programs, contracts, sales reports, sales, financial and marketing data, systems, forms, methods, procedures, and analyses, and any other proprietary information, whether communicated orally or in documentary, computerized or other tangible form, concerning the Agency's or its customers' operations and business.

Employees should ensure that any materials containing confidential or proprietary information are filed and/or locked up before leaving their work areas each day. During the workday, employees should not leave any sensitive information lying about or unguarded.

If you have any questions about this policy, consult your supervisor or the company president.

RULES OF CONDUCT AND PROGRESSIVE DISCIPLINARY PROCEDURE

There are reasonable rules of conduct which must be followed in any organization to help a group of people work together effectively. The company expects each employee to present himself or herself in a professional appearance and manner. If an employee is not considerate of others and does not observe reasonable work rules, disciplinary action will be taken.

Depending on the severity or frequency of the disciplinary problems, a verbal or written reprimand, suspension without pay, disciplinary probation, or discharge may be necessary. It is within the company's sole discretion to select the appropriate disciplinary action to be taken. Notwithstanding the availability of the various disciplinary options, the company reserves the right to discharge an employee at its discretion, with or without notice.

The following is not a complete list of offenses for which an employee may be subject to discipline, but it is illustrative of those offenses that may result in immediate discipline, up to and including dismissal, for a single offense:

1.   Excessive absenteeism or tardiness.

2.   Dishonesty, including falsification of Agency-related documents, or misrepresentation of any fact.

3.   Fighting, disorderly conduct, horseplay, or any other behavior which is dangerous or disruptive.

4.   Possession of, consumption of, or being under the influence of alcoholic beverages while on duty or client's premises or on agency business.

5.   Illegal manufacture, distribution, dispensation, sale, possession, or use of illegal drugs or un-prescribed controlled substances.

6.   Reporting for work with illegal drugs or un-prescribed controlled substances in your body.

7.   Possession of weapons, firearms, ammunition, explosives, or fireworks on Company or customer premises.

8.   Failure to promptly report a workplace injury or accident involving any of the agency's employees, clients, equipment, or property.

9.   Willful neglect of safety practices, rules, and policies.

10.   Speeding or reckless driving on agency business.

11.   Commission of a crime, or other conduct which may damage the reputation of agency.

12.   Use of profane language while on agency business.

13.   Stealing, misappropriating, or intentionally damaging property belonging to the agency or its clients or employees.

14.   Unauthorized use of the Agency's or its clients' name, logo, funds, equipment, vehicles, or property.

15.   Insubordination, including failure to comply with any work assignments or instructions given by the supervisor with the authority to do so.

16.   Violation of the Agency's Equal Employment Opportunity Policy or its Harassment Policy.

17.   Interference with the work performance of other employees.

18.   Failure to cooperate with an internal investigation, including, but not limited to, investigations of violations of these work rules.

19.   Failure to maintain the confidentiality of trade secrets or other confidential information belonging to the Agency or its clients'

20.   Failure to comply with the personnel policies and rules of the Agency.

RE-EMPLOYMENT

Former employees who are rehired and return to work within three months of their termination will not be required to go through another orientation period, unless the company deems it necessary. Former employees who are rehired and return to work more than three months after their termination will be rehired only as new employees and must complete a new orientation period. They will be considered new employees for all benefits. As a rule, the company will not rehire former employees who:

- Were dismissed by the agency
- Resigned without giving two weeks' notice
- Were dismissed for inability to perform job duties
- Had a poor attendance record
- Had a below-average evaluation
- Violated work rules or safety rules

MOONLIGHTING

The agency discourages our employees from taking additional outside employment. Employees who wish to take on outside employment must first obtain permission from the company president. Work requirements for the agency, including overtime, must take precedence over any outside employment.

The agency will not permit any employee to take an outside job with a company in the same or related business as the company, or which is in any way a competitor of the company.

If the organization permits an employee to take outside employment, the employee must report to his or her supervisor when the outside job has started. If, as a result, this moonlighting, the employee is unable to work when requested by the agency, including overtime, or is unable to maintain a high work performance level at the agency, permission to work at the outside job may be rescinded, or the employee may be subject to dismissal.

Employees are not permitted to work for any client of the company outside of the regular working hours as described above, without the express approval of the CEO or his designated representative.

The agency will not pay medical benefits for injuries or sickness resulting from employment by any employer other than the company.

BENEFITS

MOBILE PHONES

The agency will supply employees with mobile telephones as needed. The company's mobile phones are to be used for the company's business purposes only.

PAID TIME OFF

The agency provides its full-time employees with paid time off ("PTO") each year to express our appreciation and a way to renew and refresh our employees. Because our business is often very seasonal, the company reserves the right to grant PTO at times that are most suitable for our business conditions and to limit PTO during our busy season.

Full-time employees become eligible for 5 days (40 hours) of PTO per calendar year after 12 months of continuous employment with the company. After 36 months of continuous employment, employees become eligible for 10 days (80 hours) of PTO per calendar year.

Employees must use all PTO in the calendar year in which it is granted. It should be scheduled and approved by the company at least two weeks in advance. Any unused PTO will be forfeited at the end of each calendar year.

Upon termination of employment for any reason, employees forfeit any accumulated but unused PTO.

Part-time employees are not eligible for PTO.

Personal Leave

The organization may, at its discretion, grant an employee a leave of absence without pay when sufficient personal reasons necessitate such a leave. However, employees are not eligible for a personal leave of absence until they have been continuously employed as full-time employees of the company for 12 months.

The agency requires an employee to provide documentation, such as a doctor's certification of illness or disability, supporting the employee's need for a leave of absence, and the agency may periodically require the employee to provide such supporting documentation on basis during the leave of absence. Prior to or upon an employee's return to work from a leave of absence, the company may also require the employee to provide documentation establishing the employee's ability to return to work.

The agency reserves the right to determine the duration of the leave of absence, but no leave of absence shall exceed 12 weeks. If an employee fails to return to work immediately after his or her leave of absence expires, the employee will be considered to have voluntarily resigned his or her position with the company.

Employees may continue their health insurance benefits while on a leave of absence by paying the full cost of the employee portion of their premium to remain covered each month during the leave. Employees who wish to continue their insurance coverage should so advise the office manager before beginning their leave.

Leaves of absence will be without pay except that employees may be required to use any accrued paid time off during a leave. While on a leave of absence, employees will not accrue additional paid time off. Employees may be eligible for benefits during a leave under the Company's short-term and long-term disability plans.

Because operations sometimes require that vacant positions be filled, a leave of absence does not guarantee that the job will be available when the employee returns from a leave. The agency will, however, try to place you in your previous position or a comparable job which you are qualified to perform. If no such position is available, you may be eligible for rehire as a new employee if you apply for an available position for which you are qualified and if your prior work history warrants you rehire.

Bereavement Leave

The company will provide up to three days of paid bereavement leave for an employee upon the death of an immediate family member. For purposes of this policy, "immediate family" is defined as the employee's or the employee's spouse's parents, siblings, children, grandparents, grandchildren, the employee's spouse, or any other relative who resides in the employee's household.

Employees should direct all requests for Bereavement Leave to their supervisors or to the company president.

While on Bereavement Leave, an employee will be paid at straight time for the hours the employee was scheduled to work on the days missed.

Jury Leave

Employees who are called for jury duty will be granted time off with pay to perform this civic duty. Employees must notify their supervisors as soon as they learn they have been summoned as a juror so that work arrangements can be made. To be paid for Jury Leave, an employee must provide his or her supervisor with the jury summons and a note from the Clerk of the Court indicating the times the employee was in court for jury duty. The company will pay employees straight time for their regularly scheduled hours of work, minus the compensation they received from the court for their service as jurors, for up to five days of jury service. An employee who is excused from jury duty prior to the end of a regularly scheduled workday must report for work for the remainder of that day, or otherwise notify his or her supervisor of his or her availability to work.

Military Leave

The company will grant employees called into military service an unpaid leave of absence and reemployment rights as provided by the laws of the United States. Employees may use accrued paid time off during a military leave of absence, but are not required to do so.

ACKNOWLEDGEMENT OF RECEIPT OF EMPLOYEE HANDBOOK

I have received the current agency employee handbook and have read and understand the material covered. I have had the opportunity to ask questions about the policies in this handbook, and I understand that any future questions that I may have about the handbook or its contents will be answered by the Office Manager or his or her designated representative upon request. I agree to and will comply with the policies, procedures, and other guidelines set forth in the handbook. I understand that the company reserves the right to change, modify, or abolish any or all the policies, benefits, rules, and regulations contained or described in the handbook as it deems appropriate at any time, with or without notice. I acknowledge that neither the handbook nor its contents are an express or implied contract regarding my employment.

I further understand that all employees of the agency, regardless of their classification or position, are employed on an at-will basis, and their employment is terminable at the will of the employee or the agency at any time, with or without cause, and with or without notice. I have also been informed and understand that no officer, agent, representative, or employee of the agency has any authority to enter into any agreement with any applicant for employment or employee for an employment arrangement or relationship other than on an at-will basis and nothing contained in the policies, procedures, handbooks, or any other documents of the company shall in any way create an express or implied contract of employment or an employment relationship other than one on an at-will basis.

This handbook is the agency property and must be returned upon separation.

_______________________________________   _______________________________

Signature   Date

____

Employee Name: Print

REFERENCES

Arbour, S., Hambley, J., & Ho, V., (2011). Predictors and Outcome of aftercare Participation of Alcohol and Drug Users Completing Residential Treatment. *Substance use & Misuse, 46(10), 1275-1287*

Cormier, L.S. and Hackney, H. (1987). *The Professional Counselor: A Process Guide to Helping.* Englewood Cliffs, N.J. Prentice-Hall.

Decker, C.L. Scott, S.T. & Chang, V. (2013). *Developing Helping Skill: A Step-by-Step Approach to Competency.* Brooks/Cole Cengage Learning.

Desk Reference to the Diagnostic Criteria from DSM 5. American Psychiatric Association.

Eniwaye, O.O. (2014). *Theory of Time, Conflict, and the Sign of the Almighty: A Short Guide for Living.* www.Amazon.com

James, R. K. (2008). Crisis Intervention Strategies. 6th Ed. Thomson Brooks/Cole Belmont, CA.

Murphy, B. C., & Dillion, C. (2008). *Interviewing in Action in a Multicultural World.* Thomson/Brookcole. Belmont California.

Perkinson, R.R., Jongsma, A. E. Jr. & Bruce, J. T. (2014). *The Addiction Treatment Planner.* 5th Ed. Wiley. www.wiley.com/pratice/planners

Skovholt, T.M., & Rivers, D.A., (2004). *Skills and Strategies for the helping Profession.* Love Publishing Company. Denver, Colorado.

Woodside, M.R., & McClam. T. (2009). *An Introduction to Human Services.* Thomson Brooks/Cole.

About the Author:

Oludare O Eniwaye, Ph.D., HS-BCP earned a doctorate degree in Human Services from Capella University. He was an Associate Professor and Assistant Chair for the Human Services Program at Daytona State College Daytona Beach, Florida. Dr. Eniwaye has been helping people help themselves for over 15 years and has written several books and papers on addictions and other related subjects.